The
Thousand
Natural Shocks

Go for it with your writing! Russell!

Char March

Indigo Dreams Publishing

First Edition: The Thousand Natural Shocks
First published in Great Britain in 2011 by:
Indigo Dreams Publishing
132 Hinckley Road, Stoney Stanton, Leics, LE9 4LN

www.indigodreams.co.uk

ISBN 978-1-907401-45-9

British Library Cataloguing in Publication Data. A CIP record for this book can be obtained from the British Library.

Designed and typeset in Palatino Linotype by Indigo Dreams.

Cover design by Mike Barrett of www.frogsdesign.co.uk
Front cover image is 'Dark Neurons Electricity' © Tomasz Pacyna of www.pixeldreams.eu and www.dreamstime.com
Author photo © Janina Holubecki www.jholubecki.co.uk

Printed and bound in Great Britain by Imprint Academic, Exeter.

Papers used by Indigo Dreams are recyclable products made from wood grown in sustainable forests following the guidance of the Forest Stewardship Council.

The Thousand Natural Shocks... why?

The collection's title comes from Hamlet's 'To be, or not to be' soliloquy:

...and by a sleep to say we end
The heartache and the thousand natural shocks
That flesh is heir to...

Hamlet is gurning on about whether to top himself or not, but I was interested, in this collection, in exploring a whole range of shocks that the body, mind and heart are subject to as we try to make our way through the delightful obstacle course called Life. I have drawn on my own experiences as a disabled person (and my involvement in disability politics); the experiences of friends and family; on my role in taking Humanist funerals; and I have of course – being a fiction writer and playwright – made situations and characters up. I hope you enjoy engaging with all these characters, and their different takes on Life – and Death.

Char March, Hebden Bridge
September 2011
www.charmarch.co.uk

To Janina with love

Acknowledgements

Thanks so much for all the encouragement and support I've received over the years from my friends, family, fellow poets, and all the audience members who have come up to me after performances to tell me their stories. Thanks for having faith in me, and keeping on giving me a good kick up the bahookie to get my poems sent out to competitions, magazines and publishers – without all your shoving, they'd still be festering at the bottom of one of my many heaps of assorted papers! Thanks also to the magazines and anthologies who have published my work: Aireings, Albert Poets, Asylum, Bloodaxe, Chroma, Comma, Crocus, DAIL, Disability Arts Magazine, DIVA, Dreamcatcher, Envoi, Grassroots Press, Grey Hen Press, Harpies and Quines, Hens, Hot Fish Press, Indigo Dreams, Leeds Guide, Leeds Survivor Poets, Local Voices, Magma, Manchester Survivors' Press, Metropolitan, Mindwaves, Mslexia, Nomad, Onlywomen Press, Pankhurst Press, Pennine Platform, Peterloo Poets, Pitch, Prospect, Route, Sister Nose, Smith's Knoll, Survivors' Press, Templar, The New Writer, Tough Dove Books, Valid, Word Share, WWN. And finally, thank you to Sue Roberts of BBC Radio Drama for encouraging me to adapt 'The Crisis Collection' into a radio play, for doing such a splendid job of directing and producing the 'People Come Here To Cry' play, and thus opening the world of writing radio drama to me.

CONTENTS

Another box of nipples arrived today 13
The four-day wait 14
There is this silence now 15
Ridge walking 16
Après-tonsil treat 17
Eye contact 18
Washing my mother's hair 20
Award for bravery 23
On the Larbert road 24
Sticks and stones 26
Sunday 8th January 1967, 98°F 28
We were parents 33
The fruit garden remembers 34
Myxi 36
Peripheral vision 37
If I ganged oot wi' ma deid pals 39
Electric eel – grand mal 40
Dents de lion 41
A bit of a departure 42
CFS: your very own poltergeist service 44
A bit upset 45
97 ways to be Scots 46
The fitting 49
The Arkengarthdale Artemis 50
Parfum 52
There is a glass of water 54
Re-growing pinions 55
I never forget my toothbrush 56
Pearl, the allotment Viking 58

The Rex 59
I wonder what the Japanese for *Top Withens* sounds like .. 60
Do bees learn to loathe the taste of rape? 62
Sometimes little people came out of it 63
Teenage son eats honey 64
Lofty struggles with foreigners 65
3rd November 1957 66
Wings 'R' Us 70
Daedalus finds silence 71
Illegal alien 7498332 73
Forecast 74
The Crisis Collection 76
    1st visit 77
    Social Services tissues 80
    Learning the ropes 82
    Pale squares 83
    Cheese and potato gun 86
    Stock phrases 88
    Next to the box of tissues 91
    Friday runneth over 93
    Cardboard mouth 94
    The bean bag Olympiad 95
    It feels like a decision 99
    Post-script tissue 102

The
Thousand
Natural Shocks

Another box of nipples arrived today

The hospital computer's gone mad
– that's the third box this week.
You stick them on the fridge door,
the phone, the handle of the kettle.
And we laugh. Then you are sick again.

This evening you sit in your usual chair
in the bloat of chemo, your breath really
bothering you. And me, if truth be told.
You are darning pullovers neither of us
ever wear – and even Oxfam won't take.

What if I could give you a new pair?
That will always pass the pencil test, even
at 90; with velvet-dark areolae
and pert tips that jut cheekily, but
don't show through your tennis dress.

You are muttering about camels
and licking the thread for the nth time;
specs half-way down – in your usual chair.
I don't see hacked-at womanhood,
that you've sobbed salt-herring barrels for.

I see you. Darning your way to normality.

The four-day wait

The mis-shape of Ben Nevis peers
over Cow Hill and into the Chapel of Rest.

The autumn colours aren't too good
today. Defeated by the dark crimson

of the flock wallpaper. The scent of dying
bracken stubbed out by air freshener.

The bald head is thick with beige
foundation through which cold sweats

like blisters. Dad's only just been taken
out of the drawer. The man with the striped

waistcoat gives excuses in careful whispers:
a car crash at Mallaig; the ferry off because of the winds;

the only other undertaker away on holiday –
"just to Montrose." This is more seemly,

after all, than Barbados. So, Dad had to lie
in that icy drawer – a man always

paralysed by claustrophobia. While I paced
at the croft; going through the motions

with the animals – the beasts uneasy under
my city hands. And now, in this muffled room,

I stare at a cold collapse of face;
Dad long gone.

There is this silence now

The lunar calendar waxes
and wanes across the wall.

My tea ticks down in temperature,
despite my hands.

The sparrows are being polite,
the robin is wary;

the clags of soda scone
stopper their beaks –

an inedible boxful left
on the front step, with

the hundred-weight of fruitcake,
the fresh eggs, the string-tied

curly kale and the continuing
avalanche of cards

almost all saying
"at this time".

Through the kitchen window, the garden
turns its back on summer.

The washing line slices the loch,
making the tide stay out.

Ridge walking

This
is my life
out here
on this edge.

Windy here
– a narrow ridge.

Often I am scared,
have to squeeze my eyes shut,
hug myself to the rock,
crawl along on all fours
mumbling mantras.

But sometimes
I dance the thin line,
whirling in the sun,
shouting in an arms-up,
head-back laugh.

This
is my life out here.
A slim chance
with steep drops on either side,
but the views
are bloody marvellous.

Après-tonsil treat

Each shallow dish is a thick-lipped
off-white to match the slump
of vanilla – yawing in its
sweet crimson sea.

The flotilla of tinned strawberries
is furry. I am a blurred upside-down
flinching in the scratched spoon
as nurse comes at me with it – loaded.

My mouth is a sewn thing.
"Everyone loves icecream!"
She pincers my nose till I gulp.
A cheap chemical cold.

And that texture:
slime through fur –
of tiny mice turned inside-out
and left to rot in a tin tang.

Nurse bustles on, beaming.
I spit mice and blood
under my starched pillow;
tip the rest into the green lino sea.

Eye contact

They aren't allowed to use the belt anymore
– thick and animal and two-tongued,
hanging by the science lab door.
So I am sent for the eyes.

    Their jostling is wide-eyed
    their split feet, and my gutties, clumsy –
    clasping at the slick concrete.

    I share their eye-roll,
    snort with them at each percussive
    jolt of the bolt gun.

    My tongue, huge and supple,
    searches my nostrils trying
    to root out the steel tang of blood.

    The men pile them high.
    Say they can't find the lid.
    Add their guffaws.

The eyes do not wink or blink.
They are glazed over. They slither
then catch on the unlidded lip
of this stumbling bucketful
I lug up this mud slope towards
the un-mobile classrooms.

Just beyond moaning range, I set
the wobbling weight down and heave
a stream of ochre, and cloutie dumpling.
A single orb drops out
beside the language lab hut.

It stares at the red slurry
of the all-weather pitch.
Boys, raw as corned beef, thunder
on the churning rugby field
their bellows drown in the belch
from that single chimney.

Sir dishes out a scalpel,
and a spoonful of eye, each.

Mine has eyelashes and weeps rheum.
It is fish-slippy, quick as the heart
of an avocado. Still very much alive.
We are told to find the optic nerve.
I close my eyes and bayonet my thumb
to the bunsen-scarred bench.

Washing my mother's hair

It is role-reversal time:
she's bird-thin
fragile as her brittle smile
her teeth suddenly too big for her mouth
lips thinned, clumsy with Vaseline
to stop the cracks
showing.

Only last summer
she broke the world record
for Running For The Bus
carrier bags thumping at her varicose legs
then fanned herself with the Radio Times
all the fifteen stops
home.

Now her spine
is hooked
into a question mark
from which her head tries to look up.
She doesn't have to bend at all to get her hair
into the wash
basin.

For the first time
in my life, and hers,
I pour the warm water,
the baby shampoo, the best conditioner I could buy,
rub the blushing whiteness of her scalp gently
while she holds her
flannel

clamped to her eyes
like she taught me to.
And she says *Oh that's lovely.*
Just what I need, love. That's right, give it a good rub.
Oh that's just lovely. I'll be a new woman.
And I rub and chat
quietly

and joke with her in a
put-on voice:
Has Madam done her numbers for the lottery yet?
and *Will it be Torremolinos again this year, Madam?*
and the other things that mind-numbed hairdressers
say to their
ladies

and nothing at all
about how
much I love her
and how very strange it is to be feeling her wet hair
between my fingers for the very first time and how
worried I am by the
deepness

of the scoops in her neck
framed by
stirrups of collarbone and how
I've never seen her breasts before and how
surprisingly plump they are sitting on the stark
twin ladders of her
ribs.

But she still has plenty
of reserve left
and asks me to call
the nurse to see to her b.t.m. – the bedsores and the simple
wearing thin of herself. But as I help her
into a clean
nightie

I catch sight of
her mons
hairless and pink
and looking so strangely new and suddenly I'm glad
to go and get the nurse because suddenly I can't
speak and I can't
see

where I'm going
and my Mum
is dying and I've
got to come to terms with it
      and be sensible and
           look after my Dad and
                 all I want is for her to wash my hair
and
      tell me a bedtime story and
          not be
               this very old bent lady
                    with teeth that are suddenly
                       too big
                          for her mouth.

Award for bravery

The smelltaste of corridors and fingernails.
Sounds of lino coughing, rings grating
on metal rails and nurses' legs swishing busy.
The shiny thermos looks innocuous,
unstoppered becomes theatrical,
foams smoke in slovenly huffs across his desk.

The sniffing poker waitresses chink china prickly
with roses – teacups with ornate handles my Da'
can't even get his pinky through. He is in the grip
of broderie anglais, hiding his steel-capped boots,
eyeing our cakes – pushy on their EPNS stand -
all sponge fuff and hundreds & thousands.

The tiny serviette perches – useful as origami –
on his oilstained lap. He sneaks a keek
at the permed ladies buzzing with brittle chatter
and hooked pinkies, and then digs in,
wielding his cakefork like a torque wrench.
Leaning over to pour, a fairy cake welds to his breast.

He grins across at me – conspiratorial.
Cream and crumbs clot his tobacco teeth,
he clutches the mock Spode in his grime-map hands,
the same Swarfega contours that cradled me
as the Doctor's dry ice spat and sizzled
into my verruca-studded feet.

On the Larbert road

Winter
and evening coming on hard.

The loony bin looms
behind its careful belts of beeches,
fluorescent corridors stuttering.

He swings,
heavy as a bogged cow,
out into the blank road shouting.

Above the sag of shite-brown overcoat,
great tufts of newspaper
– a bizarre Elizabethan ruff –
stick out around his throat.

Ma feet ur cauld
Ma feet ur cauld

The tarmac is slimy with ice;
it smells of diesel and dead rubber.

He's stride-staggering along
clutching a couple of tatty
Fine Fare carriers
stuffed with his everything.

His boots are big
and black
and broken open.

He sinks each stride
into drunken tussocks
and dirty snow.

Ma feet ur cauld
Ma feet ur cauld

He's not thumbing,
he's not pleading,
he is commenting
on a fact
that will be with him
all winter.

Sticks and stones

They hit with a flat flop.
Didn't bounce. Seemed to sink.

Didn't bounce. Seemed to sink
a little below the surface.

A little below the surface
the dank water sounded.

The dank water sounded
thicker, like a soupy swelling.

Thicker like a soupy swelling;
a bruise echoing what?

A bruise echoing what
we realised was not a tree.

Not a tree. Not a trunk sunk;
we saw branches of arms.

Your rotted pockets' cargo lost,
you rose in anaerobic stench,

face-down. Your gloved hands
spread the evening in ink ripples.

You rolled, a log-like sleeper.
Mirrored in your open mouth –

the moon, and our horror. We dropped
our jam-jars of tiddlers and ran,

fighting each other to get home,
to get to tell – first.

Sunday 8th January 1967, 98°F

The bright orange bush flies
haven't left them, or their picnic,
alone all afternoon.

Joyce snaps the gingham tablecloth
– a ringmaster's whipcrack – twice,
three times. Determined

not to let any Blistered Grasshoppers
(that the boy finds so funny
to squeeze) back in the car.

Snap! Snap! Snap!
Like Joyce can shake Australia
out of her good English cloth.

At night Joyce knows she crawls with shieldbugs
and termites, checks the white cotton desert
every morning with a magnifying glass.

The boy is playing catch with Doug.
Or, not-catch. He is cack-handed,
"useful as an ashtray on a motorbike!".

But, even so, the ball
is the boy's favourite toy
– constantly spinning away from him.

Doug thrashes the Wallaby Grass
searching for its red orb – calls:
"I'll teach the little wowser Howzat if it kills me!"

The broad grin, the white teeth
the sun-crowed face –
Joyce turns away quickly,

stacks the pastel Tupperware
in the place she has been taught
is *"the trunk"*.

No other cars have passed
in the two hours since they stopped.
The wind is hissing like snakes

through the enclosing semi-circle
of Spotted Gum trees, through
the tinder of Brush Tail Spear Grass

and Tick Bush. By telling her their names,
Doug seems to think she will
know them, love them,

think of them as home.
She thinks: *"Why does everything
have to sound so horrid?"*

Blistered, Spotted, Spear, Tick.
The boy has, of course, started
to cry. The ball truly lost this time.

Joyce feels the prickly heat snagging
at her dress's zip. She can't even
wear a slip in this country.

Doug hauls the boy into the sky
cheering, but the boy does not stop wailing.
Burning-faced sobs;

a wild look to him. Unkempt,
savage. *"For God's sake, Doug!*
Put Geoffrey in the car!"

"Ball! Ball! Baaaaalllllllll!"
The boy is beating at the inside
of the car door, thundering

his small feet against the back
of Doug's seat. Doug pushes the lever
into Drive, the volume

is off the scale as they pull out
onto the dirt road that scratches
into heat haze.

200 yards. Joyce throws open
her door, stumbles out
running back to the clearing

already flicking at Doug's lighter:
clear this tearing grass and shrub;
find the bloody ball.

In the eye-popping sun,
the flames are unseen
then the wind breathes in,

lifts them effortless
racing through grass, shrub –
and the gum trees explode.

200-feet tapers of super-heated oil
the stench of bathroom cabinet
the eucalyptus rub her mother

smeared on her pale chest
in coal-damp Clapham.

I was writer-in-residence for Leeds Hospitals for 18 months and, while there, I worked with parents who had had miscarriages, stillborn babies or disabled babies. As well as being a writer, I also take Humanist funeral ceremonies. I wrote this poem for the parents of a stillborn child whose funeral I was taking. The parents had not only lost her, but they'd also had to go through several miscarriages. My mother had 5 late miscarriages before she was able – after taking an experimental drug – to have me. (The drug was later banned because they found it wrecks the foetus' immune system.) My story in **Some Girls' Mothers** *(Route; 2008) explores the impact of my Mum's miscarriages.*

We were parents

You played hide and seek
through our dreams for years
before you arrived.

Then, once we'd tigged you
– that squirm of blur
inside that pulsing screen –

we lay at night trying
not to giggle; straining
to hear your heartbeat.

You made us laugh a lot,
and disagree, and talk till 3am
of names, and whose nose you'd get.

And then you, who had lived
with us such a blink of time,
left.

And we are left, holding
onto nothing but naming books,
and our lurching world.

For you braced your whole
13cm self, and threw our
planet off its axis.

The fruit garden remembers

You are humming Postman Pat
as you guzzle the last of the loganberries
under the thump of the pear tree.

You are all purple tongue
and palms, your potbelly
shaking with laughter.

You yell across the lawn
holding out the windfall Russet
to Jamie and his new penknife.

Silently you squat
under his frown, and nurse
the unpeeling coil of skin.

Then, brandishing the snake,
you snatch the crisp moon from him,
and run off to your pond-side den

– to tell everything to the water-lilies.

Jamie races into the kitchen
to tell on you for not sharing
as, under your pink wellies,

the clump of iris gives way.

The pond is deep enough
for frogs to overwinter;
the sides are slick with liner.

The jam tarts need
just one more minute,
and then she'll be out.

Myxi

Such a pretty word.
It's caught in the headlights,
a crouched rumple
just out from the verge.

They swerve. It doesn't.
They pull in; click on hazards.
We get out. They fuss
in city worry. Ask

what we should do. They all
look at me. I heft
a lichened rock
from the wall. Tell them

to get back in. *Well, if that's
best then.* They jostle to lock
themselves in, keep trying
not to turn round and stare.

It's shivering.
Fur a trodden doormat
of sweat and sores.
Eyes a blank fester.

I bring the stone down
awkward on my thumb
and its head.

Peripheral vision

They flicker from room to room,
chase through the garden sprinkler,
squeal in the loftspace when I stoop
to set mousetraps, leaf through old
diaries, pick the pale blink of mushrooms
from the glow of the loamy bucket.

They peek – all glittering milkteeth
and too-large pupils – from corners.
The understairs cupboard is murmurous.
They giggle in the washbasket, eat
all the CocoPops and hide the new soap.
They watch me searching every mirror.

I stand in the shower smoothing
my seal-slick hair, my streaming face,
my unchanging outline, my conscience,
my sad mother's white hair,
my flat belly. I stand smoothing
– feeling their kick.

I grew up in Central Scotland in the 1960s and '70s and, as an English child of Yorkshire parents, learnt very quickly to develop a bullet-proof Lalland Scots accent to try to prevent getting my head kicked in. My Dad was really into folksongs, and collected hundreds of stunning Scottish ballads, marches and haunting Gaelic songs about death and loss. We used to sing these together as a family very regularly. So, when I was recently given the challenge of translating a version of Rita Boumi-Pappá's 'A Thousand Murdered Girls' poem, I turned to the harshness of my childhood accent, and that legacy of gory singing, to do it justice. Rita was a prolific Greek poet, author and translator and her poem is for the thousand women who participated in the Greek Resistance who were murdered by the Nazis. My version is for all the women killed by their partners and their families in that least safe of all places – their own homes.

If I ganged oot wi' ma deid pals

If I ganged oot fur a gander wi' ma deid pals,
the hale toon wud be stowed oot wi wheeshtit lassies.
Yon air wud be mingin' wi' corpse stank,
ilka castle an' broch wud pit thur guid white breeks
                                        oot oan sticks,
an' uvry'hin' oan uvry brae wud stap.
If I ganged oot wi ma deid pals.

If I ganged oot fur a gander wi' ma deid pals,
yous wud see wan thoosant lassies
thur burstit breests fu' wi' pain.
An' yous wud hear theym whisperin' at yous:
"How come did yous send us up the stair sae soon?
How come did yous no gless theym fit cum fur us?
Whar wur yur shivs, yur Glasgae kisses – eh?
How come did yous send us up the stair sae soon?"
Yous wud see aw that, an' hear aw that,
if I ganged oot wi ma deid pals.

If I ganged oot fur a gander wi' ma deid pals,
Theym lassies' hair wud lash aboot like flags
                                        oan the Firth.
An' Cameron Squeezebox and Black Dan the Piper
                                        wud greet
hot, salt herrin' tears – aye, baith o' theym wi sunket e'en.
A'body wud see the fu' moon gangin' awa up
        like a flo'er frae a bride's band.

An' loads ay yous men wud fa' doon deid!
If I ganged oot wi ma deid pals.

Electric eel – grand mal

It's his fifth staff meeting when
he feels its first slow slither.
That old-silver taste slurs
his tongue and the sherbet
crackles begin.

Behind his eyes things turn
acrid; his synapses bang.
There's the sticky scent
of gritted teeth and
dank river

as he goes down, the carpet
mauling his cheek.
The usual people panic;
Barbara from Reception
gaffs him with her shriek.

His muscles are a rigid jelly;
his hands and feet
fins shuddering against air –
each surge of static forcing
him further out to sea.

Dents de lion

And still they bob and buffet,
tensile strength intact.
Joyce matches me stride for stride.
The sand flubbers under our lace-ups.

Tide out. An expanse of Cleethorpes
burning with amusements.
Her grin is framed in Paisley headscarf and far out
the squint smudge of a tanker

pretending the horizon is a real place.

And still they don't scatter. My mac flaps,
my dentures clench concentration.
We moon-walk – a geriatric Chariots of Fire –
holding them aloft, hearing the stadium crowds.

Our Olympic torches: twin dandelion clocks.
Perfect spheres of fragility. One o' clock ...
heads up to the sunset. Two o'clock ...
pee-the-beds. We stride

pretending the future is a real place.

A bit of a departure

They'd spent that February morning
sifting through plant catalogues.

She chose white camellia; lemon hellebore;
four cultivars of dogwood; a daring shade
of lavender.

She ordered enough to stuff every windowbox
with heady French scent though he insisted
it set his nose off.

He ordered King Edwards, Pentland Javelin,
Giganticum onions and, in a bit of a departure,
a purple carrot.

It was that afternoon he dropped in for the results;
Monty straining on his leash, roaring at snowdrops,
and the surgery door.

When she dug them from black earth that September,
the carrots were honeycombed with larvae
despite her trying to ward off evil with interplanted garlic.

So she cooked Waitrose baby carrots in beetroot water;
presented them with the last of the parsley.
Even at that stage, he tried to eat – decided:

"Supreme Chantenay are still best."

The winter pansies, which he'd promised not to order,
arrived as she checked herself in the hall mirror
(best handbag; clean hankies for her, and the boys)

– a gross of Assorted Colours.

She waved away their stumble of sons, all
gawky with elbows. Asked the professional men,
waiting by the hearse, to load the trays all round him.

CFS: your very own poltergeist service

I smuggle myself through your customs controls.

I rifle through your muscles like acid through copper;
sabotage your mind, steal your memory,
suck your spirit out through your nostrils.

I turn down the corners of your pages, scrawl insults
in your margins, crack your spine, rip out
all your chapter endings.

I stamp on your seedlings, sow dandelion clocks
and docken, gnaw the roots off your sweet peas,
daub black spot on your roses.

I mutter at you all night, pepper your bed with itching,
nag you all day. I am dedication itself.
I never leave your side.

I hang myself round you, feel your shoulders droop.
In photographs you glimpse me: I am the ghost
of a smile somewhere very near.

*CFS is the latest term for ME – it stands for Chronic Fatigue Syndrome.
I have had CFS since 1999. Whilst working as writer-in-residence at
Leeds Hospitals, I encouraged CFS patients to think in vivid sensory
terms about their illness. They wrote a series of cracking poems using
great colours, textures, smells and tastes. These were displayed in the
CFS Clinic, and staff there had masses of positive feedback about them
from patients: "For the first time, reading these, I know someone really
understands how I feel." "It's so brilliant to give a shape, a feel, a colour
to this bloody thing that's so invisible to everyone else!"*

A bit upset
(or *Wordsworth was a cold fish*)

Perspective is the thing.
Everything is relative.
Try reflexology.
Or Reiki healing.
Or Hopi ear candles.
Or a damn good cry.
Did you know time
is a good healer?

Your hand dandles
through a book of poems.
The scrawl on the flyleaf
blows off two of your fingers.

An Indian head massage later,
a couple of prescriptions later,
a spliff and a cheeky little
Beaujolais later,
Brillo have announced
record profits.
But every cupboard is still spiked
with anti-personnel mines.
The once living room
is splattered with bits of adverb.
You've run out of nouns to throw.

You're a bit upset,
and you're not yet
recollecting it in tranquillity.

97 ways to be Scots

be Chieftain o' the Puddin' Race;
be Soor Plooms; be tablet;
be peat-smoked wild salmon; be deep-fried Mars bar;
be tartan; be leather mini-kilt;
be bunnet made o' the pie-crust;
be clarsach; be bagpipe; be crack pipe;
be Kelvinsidey; be I'm-proud-to-be-a-Scot bumper sticker;
be Castlemilk; be East Windy West Endy;
be Dunblane; be Lockerbie;
be Bannockburn; be Culloden;
be clearanced; be Wallaced and Bruced;
be Margo MacDonald;
be canni-agree-oan-the-colour-of-shite;
be Gay Gordons; be Glasgae kiss;
be Mod; be Acid House;
be Bay City Rollers; be Annie Lennox; be Shooglenifty;
be heedrum-hodrum; be Kenneth McKellar;
be Gael; be Sassenach; be Doric;
be reiver; be teuchter; be Lallans;
be Local Hero; be Braveheart; be Trainspotting;
be Black Watch; be Cameron Highlanders;
be Islay single malt; be meths and a gas canister;
be Old Firm; be shinty;
be a high heid yin; be a heidcase;
be a stoater; be a hoor;
be a jannie; be a Jessie;
be a Wee Free; be a Piskie;
be a Fenian bastard; be a Proddy bastard;
be a lad o' pairts; be a lang-luggit;
be a pan-loafie; be a numpty;

be auld claes and parritch; be in the Cabinet;
be anti-English; be European;
be abroad; be The Caledonian Society of Eastern Samoa;
be Daily Record; be Scotsman;
be Oban Times; be People's Friend;
be Monarch of the Glen; be Rab C Nesbitt;
be Jamessh Bond; be The Broons;
be a tartan tammy sewn tae a ginger wig;
be laird; be gillie; be Oor Wullie;
be having a wee dram; be puggled; be well on; be pished;
be fou; be guttered; be miraculous; be wellied; be steamin;
be fleein; be stoatin; be honkin; be stotious; be blootered;
be steamboats; be plootered; be paralytic;
be plans ganged agley

I've had alopecia since the age of 12 (as a result of the experimental drug my Mum had to take to keep me from miscarrying). I wrote this poem in anticipation of my first fitting for a wig (when I was 41). I need a wig to wear when I am meeting families to help them with their funerals, because the last thing they need to be worrying about is why the 'vicar' looks weird! In fact, my wig fitting was a total joy with a lovely NHS hairdresser (Julie Carrick) at Huddersfield Hospital – she has the best 'people skills' of anyone I've ever met in the NHS. But this poem shows something of the anxiety that alopecia can cause.

The fitting

She reaches straight over,
removes my glasses, shoves them
onto a blur that might be a shelf.

*"Now – pretend you're praying
then cup your hands out."*
She shows me the cage of her fingers

stretching the inside of the thing –
open as a handbag to receive my head.
Her damp palms earmuff me,

her fingers drag chill down my scalp.
It is far more intimate than
being fitted for any bra.

She hauls the polyester mesh,
and rubberised edge strips.
The stiff triangles of wire

are yanked down to their
"most natural position."
This seems to be my ears.

She gives a playful tousle
to my new nylon hair, sprays me
with anti-stat and Firm Hold.

Then she stands back and beams,
"There!" A very British exclamation
– one reserved for infants

or the very old.

The Arkengarthdale Artemis

Crossing these moors has to be done lightly
with a quick tripping trot for
sphagnum hummocks disguise
peaty soundings stealthy as submarines.

The ping-ping sonar of lapwings traces
from open blue to the sucking dark,
deep and brown – tender as cows' eyes.
This bog's surface is soft; yielding as an udder

licked pink and steaming by your hot rag.
For months of milking-times I lie on the lip
of Calver Clough to watch you, glistening
with steel buckets and rain, in sun and moon.

Your boots clump out your criss-crossing care,
calling your herd of ladies to you – all leggy
sweet-breathed and long-lashed. Calm
under your touch – the crown of your head

firm on their flank, they yield to you, let their
calves' milk down – into the hissing chug,
the many gulping mouths of your machines.
I lie in the tormentil on that dip slope, and I plot.

It is behind the Methodist chapel I finally bring you
to ground. I stand close by the waterbutt
to watch you tuck a wilting handful
of fox-and-cubs beside her headstone.

Then follow you into the furniture-polish-hush
of the pews. And, when enough minutes
have been spent watching your bowed head,
I huff – hard – on your bare nape.

Your tractor keys are a feeble talisman
held out like garlic. I take them, drop them
onto stone. You shift and shuffle against me;
uneasy as in an unknown stall.

But my hand's a gentle lead, and I
am breathy-warm and sure.

Parfum

At first she tries to shield herself with scent.
She moves from the frilliness of Charlie
to the mugging of Opium in a week
– but they mask nothing.

It's the bus smell – the crotch-grubby-hand-sweated-hair-snot-
with-an-undernote-of-lino-vomit – that gets to her.

So she tries daily, then twice-daily,
then hourly nose-douches of dilute TCP,
then half-strength TCP.
Within the week, it's full-strength TCP.
She nose-gargles with it for 5 minutes at a time.
It dulls nothing.

It's the tube's hogbreath
ricocheting up tiled bowels to pull her
into the gasp of thrice-breathed hot-dog fart,
with a trumpet top-note of hairspray,
that sends her to the under-sink cupboard
for the bleach.

Extra thick lemon Domestos.
She pours out two lines of its viscous pungence
then, with one of Jamie's stripy straws,
snuffs it up each nostril.
Her eyes pour bloody tears,
but her nose still bellows with smells.

Jamie skitters into the kitchen bouncing his football
– that stinks of estuaries, school furniture
and giraffes' bowels – and begs for the park.

She grabs the roll of kitchen towel,
stuffs it into her gushing nose,
snatches Jamie's hand that is putrescent cod
and pushes through the raw traffic stench
to the iron-chain-tang-pudgy-palms-on-a-rubber-swing-seat
-stamped-with-squished-dogshit-grass
all ramming into her so hard she heaves
into the litter-bin where the polystyrene-slick-of-gnawed-
chicken-legs-toxic-curry-sauce-and-Tango
cudgels her.

The brass key shrieks so loud in her door
it drowns out the lorries and Jamie's wails,
as her face smacks down
into the careful pink of the hall carpet.

It's when she wakes up,
Jamie's stink hammering at the slammed door,
and the banisters, lightbulbs, wallpaper, radiators
are immediately howling up her nose,
that she makes for the utensils drawer.
She selects the 14" kebab skewer,
stands at her reflection in the window
that chants pavements and mildewed books at her.
She brings the angled tip of the skewer
to the tip of her nose,
moves the metal arrow just inside her left nostril,
cups her right palm around the skewer's ring
– and slams the whole thing in.

There is a glass of water

Then the pills – white, innocuous.
They tell me there will be a bitterness,
but there isn't, just a faint tang
of parma violets, a few seconds
of wind through wires, before
the smell of ozone and iodine:
a beach's high-tide straggle
of bladderwrack crunch, crabshell,
the dried eggsacs of mermaids,
and a smile
easing itself
into my closing eyes.

I find it extraordinary – and hypocritical – that we are legally obliged to treat our dying animals better than we are allowed to treat ourselves. Why can't we, as human beings, be allowed to die when – and where – we choose to? How many of us actually want to end our days on a Swiss industrial estate?

Re-growing pinions

She's had anal sex
and rather liked it.
She scoffs baby new potatoes,
that you scorned, they squeak
round her teeth like wax eyes.
She lugs in occasional armfuls
of those lilies that made you choke.

On Sunday mornings there is
no Radio 2. She kayaks and
has buried the cat you left –
he was dead, just.
She sucks tuna straight
from the tin; has never made
another Swiss roll; took E
for her 56th; sings Bessie Smith
on the loo – the door never shut.

The herpes you gave her
erupts every few months
but now she doesn't interrogate
the steamed mirror with panda
eyes – she swallows Lysine,
is careful of her nut intake.

I never forget my toothbrush
(in honour of Jonathan)

She squeezes the tube
but the rest I do myself.

They've wrapped the handle in thick, blue foam
to make it easy for me to hold.

I grasp it firmly.

She encourages me to watch myself
in the liver-spotted mirror. She calls it:

"hand/eye co-ordination orientation" and
"building a positive relationship with your self-image"

I just like to see I'm still visible.

Sometimes she leaves me all by myself to do it.
Those are the best days.

Today she hovers. Wiping quickly round the bath;
ripping open more toilet rolls – all her movements over-rapid.

Her mouth is a cartoon – a single, thin line
saying: martyr.

I zone her out and wave briefly to myself
with the toothbrush on its way to my gnashers.

My grin is yellow and smelly, but Enter Right
the sliding, gritty mint;

the white, foaming drool
that I am allowed to gob.

I champ and froth, and imagine myself rising
over the last fence at the Grand National

ahead by three lengths
and no need for a bloody jockey.

Pearl, the allotment Viking

We wrench at the crusty boards;
a crackle of turquoise paint and crazed
rust. The two deckchairs are locked
in an elbowed embrace that tears apart,
fluttering rotted stripes
– like an ancient battleflag
going down under hooves.

The spitting blaze is a baresark beacon
against the shutting down of November.
The leaning towers of sprouts, the young leeks,
the left-to-seed parsley flap in the flaring wind.
Sodden earth clubs our wellies
as we heave planks loose
– stoke the Valhalla flames.

Pearl's shed lurches forward onto its knees
– an old warrior axed from behind.
Its burning gasps force us back.
This was the shed's last summer
as Pearl's longboat. Humping heavy,
as over uneven swell, it swayed and creaked
through August evenings as,

another good afternoon's weeding behind her,
Pearl pulled the little nets on the single porthole,
and got down to it with Stan.
His zimmer frame hung from a nail outside
– a gleaming set of horns hacked
from some mythic beast.
His wife safely bedridden.

The Rex

It was 1962, in Anstruther,
with Auntie Eileen who snorted
when she spoke. I wore my floppy velvet
hat that I refused to use fleaspray on
and she had on her dung-yard wellies so
not many sat near us. And the rest
moved when we brought out our sardines
and started cracking the boiled eggs
on the armrests. And the place emptied
when she opened up in her opera baritone
about cunnilingus not being great
when Morag had just done an all-nighter
in the lambing shed. I slept through the film
– something with David Niven in, as ever –
my head cushioned against her missing
left breast, the armrest welding in
like another rib. *Barbour* was embossed
backwards on my cheek when I woke – her
carrying me up the back-lanes home.

I wonder what the Japanese
for *Top Withens* sounds like

Today a 67-year-old woman
from Nagasaki wept

on my shoulder, sobbing out to me
her longing to stand here since,

age 13, she had devoured
Wuthering Heights, hearing

the moor wind, and Cathy's longing,
in the sound of Shinto temple bells

and the parping traffic
on the Shianbashi road.

We stand today, my arm around
her tiny waist, as she dabs her eyes

and smiles and smiles
and we listen, together,

to the bubbling trills of curlew above
and the heavy breath below of

The Keighley and Worth Valley steam train
and to Kate Bush warbling from the Bronte Balti House.

I pull my blissed-out companion
onto the narrow gritstone pavement

as gaudy mountain bikers judder
down the cobbles where cholera flowed

in Branwell's day, and the apothecary
didn't sell retro pinnies,

but raw opium to ignite his dreams
of knocking his sisters' talents

into an early grave.

Do bees learn to loathe the taste of rape?

I stand gasping inside the cloy of black netting,
sucking in the sweet smoke – as much to try
to calm myself, as drowse them.

They crawl in front of my myopia, black-hair-legs poking
through the mesh. Then stare their compound image
of me back into the mind of hives.

I become soporific, tuning into their insect
leg-language, the cleaning of their antennae,
their modulating rhythms of humbuzz.

I never take much of their honey. Derek has started
grumbling about the falling yield – talks about:
"setting a fire under the buggers".

So I've taken to checking out offers on runny honey
in Lidl and Aldi. Back in the jarring-shed, the cool brick
all around me blooming with rings of white salts,

I am magician.

Our yield climbs up the shining jars, as I mix
the German bees' Honig with our Norfolk's
– ours so much yellower, so much like the sunshine

that pushes in through the cobwebbed window, so much
like the thunder-bug-filled miles of swaying gold
that stretch to all my horizons.

Sometimes little people came out of it

Or a bird.
A wooden bird
with a bright-painted tongue.

It was round
and it was on the wall
above the piano.

It told me when to eat
and when to go to bed.
It was on my wrist as well.

It had hands.
And a heartbeat if you listened
with your good ear.

We don't have it anymore.
Not here.
They say we don't need it now.

Oh, is it time already?

Teenage son eats honey

A veiled man stole it
in the choking confusion of smoke;

cut waxy chunks heavy with scent
from the clagged ochre of the frames;

whirred them with the steady sound
of pigeon wings in a steel drum;

ran the amber into each fat jar.

You sit picking at yourself

with stubbed fingers that smell
of Marlboro and your last wank.

I spread pupae-fuel on your toast;
the thrum of a thousand insects.

Behind your blank eyes
fizzes the furious hormonal hive.

Lofty struggles with foreigners

They won't open the bleedin' patio doors.
I'm not used to this sort of treatment, me.
I'm a bleedin' champion. I'm not stopping out here.
They're all riff-raff. Bleedin' tits, and seagulls – I ask you.
And they all talk foreign. God knows where I've ended up.

Those sidewinds were an absolute B. Eric'll be worried sick.
White bread?! White bread? What do they think I am?
Geroff me! Jeez, there's no need to pull my bleedin' leg off.
Just read it! *"Oh, Archie, his wee hairt is aw thundering."*
Tell me about it! Oh, reading glasses – at bleedin' last.

Well, go on! Ring him up then. He'll be pacing about,
slugging back Milk of Mag with Doreen whittering
"Come on in and keep warm, ducks. He'll be fine I tell you."
Bet some of them Halesowen lads'll be home and dry.
Cracked eggs the lot of them – and pigeon-chested.

A box in the woodshed?! A box in the bleedin' woodshed?
Eric'll not be happy. But least he's told them about
The Necessity of Mixed Seeds and Best Butter. More like
Tesco's own brand, actually. And no hot water bottle!
How do they expect a champ like me to recuperate?

Rain – again? What a country! Mind, that hot porridge,
that wasn't half bad. So, Flight Checks Complete,
as Eric says. *Ta very much then…..I says: Ta Very Much.*
Oh, never mind. Just smile and nod – always best with
foreigners, Eric says. … Well, come on – chuck us up then!
Talk about dim.

3rd November 1957

My name is Barker.
I am in my new harness.
This is my new bag.
This is my new kennel.
It looks very small.
It smells strange.
Vladimir throws a BIG blob of gel
into my new kennel.
I jumps inside!
Gel lovely squelchy yummy;
I lick and lick, lick and lick!
Lots of hands busybusy.
They put wires in my new harness,
and in the walls of my new kennel.
Then chains – big heavy chains.
Hold me tighttight to corners
of my new kennel.
Then CLANGBANG!
They shut door.
I use my name again and again
but they do not open the door.
I slurpyslurpy up the gel.
Sudden, there is hugebig ROAR.
I use my name.
Put tail between legs.
It hugs my new bag.
I use my name.
I use my name.

I curl up. Try to be smalltiny.

But it hard to lie down,
chains pullpull.
The roar not go away.

I see a eye – a one eye.
It watching me.
Sometimes it blink.
I try to stand up,
try to lick the eye.
Try. Try.
Not reach.

Eye not smack me,
not speak to me.

The roar it go on on on.

My harness tight.
It get hothot.

Bag full of poo.
It leak all over me.
Badbad smell.
Hate bag – bitebitebite!
Now me lie all in poo.

Sucksucksuck at little pipe
like Vladimir taught me
but no water come now.

No more yummy gel.
That pipe all squeakywhistley now.

Hot. Tired. Hot.

Eye blink at me.
Harness tight.
It has bited my legs.

Me use my name only sometimes.

Eye blink at me.
Me hothot.
Me drink pee.
Kennel hothot.
It smellysmellysmelly.

Me chewchew tight harness.
Me bited leg.
It sore big and badbad smell.
Me dirty hothot.
All is badbad smell.

Where Vladimir?

Eye blink at me.
Then man speak!
"Today, comrades, is the 40th anniversary…"
Jumpy up, legs shakeshake
me wobblyweak, but wagwagwag!
Me try to use my name.
"…of our Glorious Revolution… "

Man went all crackle.

Just me now.
Just me.

Me can't use name.

All hot.

Hot.

Laika means Barker. She was a 3-year-old stray dog that the Soviets trained for their space programme. She survived for 4 days in Sputnik 2 – watched by a TV camera. Dr Vladimir Yazdovsky was one of the scientists who trained her. Just before the launch, he took Laika home to play with his children. He wrote, "I wanted to do something nice for her: she had so little time left to live." Laika died of overheating. Her body orbited Earth another 2,570 times before Sputnik 2 broke up on re-entering Earth's atmosphere on April 14, 1958.

Wings 'R' Us

Yeah, like, Dad's always been, like, an airhead, right?
Drives Mum nuts. All his wacky get-bling-quick schemes.
Latest's gone pear-shaped – as per. So we gotta fly.
I mean, literal, man. He's been hoarding loo-roll tubes,
lengths of elastic, bits of candle for, like, weeks.
*Oh, and taking this weird interest in, like, **hens**.*

I mean, all he's gotta do is gimme the nod.
I txt some of the gang to, like, ramraid us outta here.
But Dad always has shedloads of, like, conspiracy theories.
Latest is this king fella we just done this garden re-design for?
(Kindofa neat maze for some truly wild beastie of his.)
Anyhow, now Dad says that Mr-Crown-guy wants to pop us.

So, like, we're gonna wing it. Sounds groovy.
Straight off this big fucker of a cliff. Wish I could invite the guys,
y'know, have a few spliffs, a crate of Stella for the big off.
But Dad's real into his wacko groove: strict Need To Know basis.
Mum skyped "humour him". But he's all yak-yak in my face!
Zeus! Less of the instructions already, eh Pops?
*You'd think **I** was the airhead around here – duh!*

Daedalus finds silence

You're on something.
You're too keen, too compliant, too...
"hot" I'm sure you'd say.
I say: *"Harder can't you!*

Don't cross the threads!
Keep the strain even!"
Snapping, and not
meaning to – as usual.

Everything is creaking,
even your beatific smile.
We climb inside our flimsy birds.
I start my final checks.

You screw your tch-tch earphones in,
yawn, don't watch for my signal, but
we are soaring. I am astonished.
You, simply delighted.

I envy you so many things,
but particularly this –
your sheer certainty
in life. And, strangely, in me.

All James Dean hair and smoke,
you puff out bliss and lounge back,
basking in the rising thermals
till you are dot; my shouts, silence.

You whoop down, all grin and slicked hair
"Hey – lighten up, Dad!"
But your victory loop's a torque too far
for tender wing-trim.

I yell a centre of gravity.
Then watch as your fingers
scrabble a hold – on nothing
but your vanishing smile.

At the border they empty my pockets.
I have to refuse to help,
for I must concentrate,
on carrying you –

salt-gentle and glimmering
in the gowpen of my hands.

Illegal alien 7498332

- one 4D pencil nub, badly chewed;
- one golfball-sized lump of brown substance
  wrapped in kitchen foil
  (Note: Subsequent lab report shows this to be
  human ear wax.);
- one key-ring ornament of small plastic bull;
- one compass – tampered with
  (fitted with lodestone to show inaccurate North);
- one half-tube fruit Polos
  (sent for analysis – report awaited);
- two IMAX ticket stubs for 'The Wonder of Flight';
- one toothpick – wooden, broken.

No documents;
no apparent means of support;
incoherent when questioned;
talks of 'son' but no sponsoring address given;
could be Greek?
No record of DNA on database.
Violently refused samples from liquid he held
in cupped hands.
This appears to be salt water,
but lab warned could be nitro-glycerine.

Entrance refused.

Forecast

Well, and wasn't it a lovely weekend?
Largely conflict-free with ceasefires and
negotiations breaking through in most areas,
but still that odd risk of friendly fire on high ground.

However, as we look ahead to this week
it's not quite such a settled picture.
By Tuesday, things will be hotting up with some
quite nasty patches of cluster bombs in the South West.

A smattering of Smart bombs will push collateral damage
up around Birmingham. And that will be followed
by a slow-moving trough of high level fall-out.
This will bring with it a risk of burning,

so do remember your premium-factor radiation cream.
A heavy ground frost in the North might make
gravedigging difficult on Thursday. And there's
a further risk of patchy missiles on low-lying ground,

so do take care if you are out and about.
However, the pattern of rather intense fronts
we've been having lately will be moving away
towards the continent by the end of the week.

And the summary for the Home Counties: Bullets,
brisk at times, especially later. Moderate casualties,
becoming heavier. But brief spells of calm breaking
through here and there, just in time for the weekend.

The Crisis Collection

I adapted this series of poems into an award-winning BBC Radio 4 play ('People Come Here To Cry'), and also a stage play that was toured successfully by Red Ladder and staged to critical acclaim at West Yorkshire Playhouse. It is based on my own experiences of trying to get help from the counselling industry. I have been active in the Survivors' Poetry Movement for many years, and really value the integrity, insightfulness and ace sense of humour of the survivors I have met. My sense of humour is, quite definitely, the only thing that's kept me alive – thank goodness we can laugh, especially at our bleakest times!

1st visit

I understand this place
is experi-mental.
Amusing term really,
considering.

One of the first in the country.
So, Barnsley leads the way
in something other
than the lamb chop then.

The room is stale
with cigarette smoke.
I am standing by the open window
to avoid sucking into myself
the previous client's
exhaled despair.
Below, the garden is bright:
a municipal green;
as nurtured
as a roundabout.

She hurries in
– quietly,
for she is a well-trained
professional –
with the wastepaper bin
emptied of crumpled tears.

She closes the door,
quietly,

and smiles at me
over the top of her glasses,
as if shy,
making it clear
that she's not expecting
anything
of me.
And that this is
my own time,
and that she is ready
as a *sounding board.*

She resonates
professional concern
for me to be
at my ease.
I am now supposed to be ready to begin.

One hour later
I am supposed to be ready
to stop.
To go,
quietly,
and preferably without tears.

She uses my first name
three times
on the short walk downstairs.
Tries to appear at ease
with not letting me inside their
Office - Private
while she juggles the large diary

and the doorstop
and I am *slotted-in*
for another
session.

Then it is time for her to use
my first name again
– twice
in the same sentence –
and to try to decide whether
it would be
invading my personal space
to touch me on the arm
or even to give me
a brief hug
as we part at the inner door
that says
Please Ring The Bell.

I close the outer door behind me,
an anonymous blue.
No number.
No name plaque.
No CRISIS CENTRE
in big bold red and gold winking neon
to cheer the bloody place up.

Social Services tissues

I've been in two of the
Counselling Rooms
now.
Both have two uneasy chairs
and a low coffee table,
although we always drink tea.

On the table in each room
is a cheap aluminium ashtray
– weightless.
For the security of staff
I presume on my second visit
when I'm a bit more able
to take in
my surroundings.

And a box of tissues.

I had thought they would hide these.
Have them in a drawer
to pull forth
like a string of bright
magician's handkerchiefs
when a **CRISIS** loomed
but no, they sit there
waiting,
expecting.

The expectation of the whole place
is that people will want

to be miserable here.
By my fourth visit, this has got to me.
I want to arrive in bowler hat,
tails and a cane
and clatter-tap my way
across the gloomy Social Services' hallway
and up the badly-carpeted stairs
singing some crass musical number.

Learning the ropes

Today I sit huddled
and sobbing
on the hearth rug in
The Quiet Room.
This makes me feel
incredibly secure.
It's exactly the sort of thing
loonies do.
I'm not proving at all good
at being normal
– failure pretty much all round,
but I'm learning the ropes here
quickly.

Last week I caught myself rocking
backwards and forwards
in my chair,
moaning
– just like a *real* nutter.

Pale squares

On each door
of each room
– hung from a length of string –
there is a flimsy, pastel-coloured card.
Very Primary-schoolish.
Pale green.
Pale blue.
Watery yellow.
Nothing too dramatic.
No red rag,
to the bulls.
Wouldn't fit
with the washed-out,
wept-into texture
of the place.

Someone,
who fancies themself
as a dab hand at writing notices,
has scribed on each card
in everso affected, curly wurly, oogly woogly,
this-won't-look-too-officious-if-I-write-it-like-a-7-year-old-
doing-joined-up-writing-for-the-first-time
the room's name:

Office – Private
The Quiet Room
(which has a large television)
The Reading Room
(which doesn't have any books)

Kitchen
Counselling Room 1
Counselling Room 2
(there are more on the next floor,
but we haven't ventured up there yet)
Toilet
(there is a line of these,
so actually it is:)
Toilet Toilet Toilet Toilet
Bathroom

Yes, there's a *Bathroom* here.
Literally a room with a bath in it:
a huge, high-sided, cast-iron bath
set up on ugly legs.
And a towel rail,
and that's it.
Very Social Services.
Very Health Service.
Very weird.
People come here to talk.
But obviously
we must be cleaned thoroughly;
as if we're not all washed
almost transparent
by our tears.

I hate the *Bathroom*
and find it very sinister.
I always go to the
Toilet
furthest away from it.

I imagine white-coated
Bathroom Attendants,
pulling on surgical gloves,
emerging from it,
waiting outside
the *Toilet* door
for me.

There,
that sounds suitably barmy
doesn't it?
I told you I was
learning the ropes.

Cheese and potato gun

I find myself doing this now:
thinking in terms
of them
and us.

I was feeling sorry
for the scrawny lass
that sees me.
My *PCC.*
Personal Crisis Counsellor.
She always seems
to be having to work
through her dinnerbreaks
because of people running over.
So I bought a couple
of cheez 'n' tayto pasties.
from that place in the market
with the eccentric spelling.
I reckoned my *PCC* was a vegetarian
– she looks like one.
A bit peaky.
So, today I presented her
with my offering.
And she looked at me
like I'd just pulled a gun.

"Oh no.
I couldn't possibly accept a gift
– from a client".
So, hers had to sit

by the box of tissues,
steaming.
I had it for my tea that night
with some sprouts.
But I realised the lines
had been made clear
– drawn up.
Them
and us.

Stock phrases

Hitler always used green ink.
I read that somewhere.
I haven't told her that of course.
She might think I was getting at her.
But it gets in the way somehow.
I find I'm watching her
– squeaking away in green –
and she's probably thinking
what a calming colour green is.
And my mouth just fills with this need
to tell her about Hitler.

I come out of each session,
and almost straight away
I can't remember what on earth got said
– by me that is.
I hear her words
for days afterwards.
Like a strange bell – tolling away.
But that's probably just the repetition.
She always seems to say the same things
– Stock Phrases – I've started to call them.
I've given them numbers.

Today I asked if I could see
what she was writing.
It just popped out.
I suppose it bothers me.
Her so earnestly hunched over her pad,
squeaking away with her green felt tip

on the pale yellow pad.

Anyway, she looked up from her pad.
Looked at me,
over the top of her glasses
with that slightly startled
– rabbit-in-the-headlights –
look of hers.

She struggled around for a bit
– probably trying to find a Stock Phrase
that fitted the situation.
Then she smiled and said
that she just wanted to make sure
she remembered
the chronology of my history.

Well, I'm not likely to forget it
– if you need reminding, I said.

She gave me her best, concerned look then
and carefully stowed the yellow pad
and her green pen
inside her brown folder and said
that *really, time was up for today,*
(Stock Phrase number 9)
and *was that okay with me?*
(Stock Phrase number 3).

No, I think we should
work on this issue
right through the night.

I feel it
requires a lot of concentrated, quality time,
I said.

But I didn't say this
till I was standing at the bus-stop
on Cleveland Street
and I got some funny looks
from the woman in front of me.
But then, I had told her
she had a ladder in her tights,
so she probably wasn't predisposed
towards me doing
a bit of open sharing
with her.

Next to the box of tissues

Don't these professionals know
how frustrating it is
to throw something weightless?
Like a cheap aluminium ashtray.

If you feel the need to *throw* something
then it is a real need
for a dramatic gesture.
Not the awkward flight
of an aluminium ashtray
that is diverted from hitting the wall
by the draught of it being thrown,
and swings back at you
– like a mini Frisbee –
to tinkle against the leg
of your chair
and then rolls away,
lopsidedly round and round,
to come to rest,
not even upside down,
under the table.

Just makes you feel silly
and feel that you look silly
and may even make it more likely
that you pick up something else.
The coffee table for example.
Or the Counsellor.
And lob them through the window.
A much more satisfying sound

than the tinkle
of a cheap aluminium ashtray
and the gentle drift
of cigarette ash
floating in a lazy trail
from its erratic flightpath.

I haven't even thrown
a damp tissue
in the bin
– yet.
Let alone
an ashtray
or a Counsellor
out the window.

As I said, I'm only just
learning the ropes.

Friday runneth over

It's Friday.
I don't know why I know that,
but I do.
I'm waiting for her
as usual.
Her Friday client
always runs over.

Runs over what?
The dog on the way here?
Or maybe it's their cup.
You know:
"My cup runneth over".
She must get through
a lot of tissues
when that happens.

Her Tuesday client
runs over too.
So I suppose it could be Tuesday,
but I know it's not.

I try not to.
Run over I mean.
I've bought this
little electronic alarm.
Quite fiddly to set.
I have it going off
three minutes
before she calls time:
just enough for me to get tidy.

Cardboard mouth

It irritates her
that I don't use their, specially-provided,
Social-Services-approved tissues.
I always bring my own hankies.
Their over-washed cotton
is kinder to my poor nose and eyes.
Sometimes I don't bring enough.
Maybe I haven't done the washing for a few days,
or I have a particularly wet session.
And then she presses forward
with the white-and-grey-striped box,
pleased to be of professional help.
Satisfied in her role at last.

And yet, she never just pulls one out,
hands me it.
I find it difficult enough
to even see the box,
when my specs lie sodden
on the coffee table,
let alone find
the cardboard mouth
the edge of a white white tissue.

At least they don't say
Man-Sized.

Then I think I'd *have*
to throw something.

The bean bag Olympiad

It is bright red
– an unknown colour
in this pastel place –
and brand new.
It slumps in the corner,
a sulk of polystyrene beads.
Its loop of fabric handle
cocked like a lone ear.

There's one in each of the
Counselling Rooms.
I'd thought they were
for kiddies –
to play on.

But no.
She offered it to me today
– to hit –
instead of the wall,
the windowframe,
myself.

These professionals
really haven't grasped
that self-harm is *exactly*
what some of us want to do.

They might find it hard to cope with,
I mean, what sort of a caring image
does it put out about a place

that has its clients walking away
with bruised heads and bleeding hands,
from beating at the walls
and themselves?

But a bleeding hand
is so much easier
to bandage, heal, cosset,
feel compassion for,
than a broken mind.

And I crave
a simplicity
of healing.

I know *she* has an image of me
crawling,
sobbing,
across the nylon fawn of the carpet
to beat at the red ineffectually
with wayward swings
of my arms.
Quickly tiring.
Slower and slower.
Then sinking
into a heap
beside it
– a sob bag.

I have an image of me
in an enormous stadium
– cheering crowds,

sunshine,
huge TV screens,
intense commentary
in umpteen languages
outlining my previous achievements
at this event.

A hush
as I step forward
to liberally chalk my hands.

I am dressed
in dazzling lycra.
I saunter up to the bean bag,
spit on my palms,
brace myself,
bend my knees,
grasp the handle

and swing swing swing

and release

with a huge grunt.

Freeze-frame on me
– grinning,
exuberant,
arms up to the crowd
while the commentators scream:
"New Olympic and World record!"
"Maximum points for style and grace,
so important,

in the women's events"
as the red dot
of the bean bag
disappears
out over the West stands,
past the Olympic flame
and still rising.

It feels like a decision

It's not a good day today.
I'm sat on the floor,
in the corner
of *Counselling Room 2*,
sobbing and aching
and trying to stifle screams.

She is perched forward on her chair
her notepad pulled up close
to her small bosom.

"I feel..... you are very..... angry"
she says at last.

Silence
– apart from the thud
of my head
on plaster.

Silence.

Five minutes on:
"Do you want to......... talk.........
about your......... anger?"

And something just gives.

"What makes you so convinced I'm angry?"

And I get up

in a single, clean motion.

It feels like a decision.

"Wait here" I say.
And I walk out,
quietly closing the door.

I stand for a moment in the corridor,
wondering what I am doing.
I only know that I can't take that room,
her questions,
this whole regurgitation
of pain on demand
anymore.

I take the stairs down
three at a time,
grab two of the ugly hall chairs
and prop open the inner door
– **Please Ring The Bell** –
and the anonymous blue outer one.

A sweet breeze
blows up the garden
and into the Social Services' air.
I walk out.
Down the steps,
across the lawn
– frightened at walking away
from this *'help'*;
terrified of what it will do to me

if I keep coming back.

At the gate I turn left, up the hill.
For the first time in my life
I consciously litter
– releasing balls of crumpled tears
from my hands.
Little blobs of sadness
bouncing along the pavement and gutter.
They look quite jolly.

As glad as me
to get the hell out.

Post-script tissue

Inside
she waits
for five minutes,
writes a note
in careful green lettering
in the pale yellow file.

Then,
quietly,
unlocks the tissue cupboard.
For there are
others
to be seen.

Always others
to be seen
– handed tissues.

Indigo Dreams Publishing
132 Hinckley Road
Stoney Stanton
Leicestershire
LE9 4LN